Prophetic Boot Camp

Basic Training for the 21st Century

Sherry Anderson

CONTENTS

ACKNOWLEDGMENTS

I thank You, Lord, for Your amazing grace and faithfulness!

Thank you, Mike, for your continued love and support in my pursuit of God and writing.

To my writing intercessors: I am so grateful for your help on this project.

INTRODUCTION

What is the purpose of *Prophetic Boot Camp*? It is for anyone who wants to learn the basics about the prophetic: what it is, who can participate, how to receive a prophecy, and what to do with it. It is to clear up some wrong ideas and to show the difference in the prophetic *gifting* and prophetic *call*, the difference between psychics and prophets, and to introduce many different expressions of God speaking to us. Another reason for this manual is to share the wisdom that I have gained through experience. This wisdom came by stumbling forward and making nearly all the mistakes that could be made. There are valuable lessons that I will share that can save a teachable person much pain and misunderstanding.

We are living in a prophetic age. The Lord said in His Word, *And afterward* [in the last days], *I will pour out My Spirit on all people. Your sons and daughters will prophesy, your old men will dream dreams, your young men will see visions. Even on My servants, both men and women, I will pour out My Spirit in those days.* (Joel 2:28-29) I formerly thought God was referring to pouring His Spirit on Christians, but the expression He used was "all flesh" or "all people." There is a spiritual hunger and awareness of the supernatural that is being released to the non-believers. This is evidenced by the number of people seeking help through psychics and New Age avenues. Recently I was in Barnes & Noble Bookseller. The book section dealing with the supernatural, occult, New Age, fortune telling, spells, and such as that was close to the size dedicated to authentic Christianity. The enemy is making the most of the spiritual hunger by deceiving people and drawing them into darkness. God is calling the Church to step up and be the *real deal* in a world of counterfeits.

God is looking for a harvest of souls and is communicating through dreams in an unprecedented way to both believers *and* non-believers. Prophetic people have a crucial role to play in this hour that we live. As with the unsaved people such as Pharaoh of Egypt and Nebuchadnezzar, king of Babylon, there is a need for people like Joseph and Daniel to have understanding in visions and dreams.

In the past, the focus has only been what we can do to serve the Lord in the Church. In the days to come, the prophetic gifting will be used right out there where we live. God desires to speak in the workplace, the medical field, the education system, the military, the government, and wherever people interact and gather. *The earth is the Lord's, and everything in it, the world, and all who live in it.* (Psalm 24:1) He has a right and a reason to be speaking. It all belongs to Him!

This is an exciting day to be alive! Prophets and prophetic people will find their gifting is greatly needed.

1

WHAT IS THE DIFFERENCE BETWEEN THE GIFT OF PROPHECY AND THE OFFICE OF A PROPHET?

The Gift of Prophecy

In the 13th chapter of 1 Corinthians, there is an excellent treatise on love. It is immediately followed in chapter 14 with the exhortation to *follow the way of love and eagerly desire spiritual gifts, especially the* **gift** *of prophecy.* Paul encourages the church at Corinth to continue praying in tongues to edify themselves and speak to God, but expresses how much more important the gift of prophecy is when they assemble together. This is a letter that was written to the whole Church, not just a few people that were in a prophetic class. It would be good to expand your vision here to realize that you do not need a "special" calling to operate in this gift. *But everyone who prophesies speaks to men for their strengthening, encouragement and comfort. He who speaks in a tongue edifies*

1

himself, but he who prophesies edifies the church. I would like every one of you to speak in tongues, **but I would rather have you prophesy.** (1 Corinthians 14:4-5)

Not everyone who prophesies is a prophet or being developed by God to be one. Every believer can have this gift. The gift of prophecy is listed in 1 Corinthians 12 along with other spiritual gifts. Even though the gifts are listed separately in these Scriptures, it is possible for all the gifts to operate through us as we grow in faith and the Holy Spirit determines the need.

The Office of a Prophet

The office of a prophet is part of what is commonly called five-fold ministry. That phrase was coined to identify callings to particular offices in the Church that are listed in Ephesians 4:11-12a. *It was He* [God] *who gave some to be apostles, some to be prophets, some to be evangelists, and some to be pastors and teachers, to prepare God's people for works of service...* These five types of leaders are to equip and train God's people to do the work of ministry, much of which will take place outside of the Church.

The prophet Jeremiah's call and job description are found in Jeremiah 1:5-10. *"Before I formed you in the womb I knew you, before you were born I set you apart;* **I appointed you as a prophet to the nations.***" "Ah, Sovereign Lord,"* I said, *"I do not know how to speak; I am only a child."*

*But the Lord said to me, "Do not say, 'I am only a child.' You must go to everyone I send you to and say whatever I command you. Do not be afraid of them, for I am with you and will rescue you," declares the Lord. Then the Lord reached out His hand and touched my mouth and said to me, "Now, I have put My words in your mouth. See, today **I appoint you over nations and kingdoms to uproot and tear down, to destroy and overthrow, to build and to plant."***

Based on this, prophets will:

- Root out – error and uproot things that flourished in the last move of God but are not productive anymore.

- Pull down – any thought that doesn't agree with the truth of God's Word.

- Destroy – strongholds.

- Overthrow – the enemy's plans.

- Build – God's kingdom.

- Plant – good seed.

Following is a quote from Graham Cooke, a prophet from England: "It takes years to make a prophet. The journey is necessarily tough.

Only the called and the committed will pass the tests required to stand before the Lord as a true spokesperson of His intent. It takes seasoning and refining. Maturity is not about time served, but being well versed in the ways of God."

Much of what we have dealt with concerning prophets has been with mistakes made by budding prophets. Because of lack of training and mentoring, budding prophets have not known what to do with the revelation God has given them. Since prophets are intercessors, much of what God reveals to them is to pray about. I used to think that I was supposed to tell whatever God showed me.

Mistakes made by budding or immature prophetic people have ended up causing confusion to others and rejection for themselves. However, before we stone them, we must admit they are not the only ones in the five-fold ministry that have made mistakes, or caused confusion and damage to believers.

If a prophet is known to be submitted to the lordship of Jesus Christ, is part of a local body of believers, and accountable to his/her pastor, their part in building the local church and the kingdom of God needs to be embraced and welcomed if we want to receive a prophet's reward. The reward is to receive benefit of the blessing their ministry can bring to us. As it says in Matthew 10:41, *Anyone who receives a prophet because he is a prophet will receive a prophet's reward.*

Prophets cannot be controlled. If they are controlled, they cease to be God's voice.

First of all, after the above statement, I need to clarify something. The Bible teaches that *the spirits of prophets are subject to the control of prophets.* (1 Corinthians 14:32) The Living Bible translation says it even more plainly: *Remember that a person who has a message from God has the power to stop himself or wait his turn.* A prophet *can* control himself.

What I am referring to is about controlling MATURE prophets and what they have to say. If we limit them to the standard of the *gift of prophecy* (i.e., it must exhort, edify, or encourage), we will miss the benefit of the office of the prophet. We must be open to hear what God wants to say through them.

Consider the following story: in 1 Kings 22, King Ahab and King Jehoshaphat needed to hear from God as to whether to go to war to retake some land. Ahab called his 400 prophets and they all said to go. *Jehoshaphat asked, "Is there not a prophet of the Lord here whom we can inquire of?"* The king of Israel answered Jehoshaphat, "There is still one man through whom we can inquire of the Lord, but I hate him because he never prophesies anything good about me, but always bad. He is Micaiah son of Imlah." They summoned Micaiah. They were dressed in their royal robes, and all the prophets were prophesying before them and it got quite dramatic. Zedekiah (a prophet) had made iron horns and told them that God said they would gore the enemy until he is destroyed with the horns. All the other prophets prophesied the same thing, promising victory. The messenger who had gone to get Micaiah told him to agree with what all the other prophets were saying. *But Micaiah said, "As surely as the Lord lives, I can tell him only what the Lord tells me."* However, when he arrived, his advice to the king was to attack and that God would give him victory. *The king said to him, "How many times must I make you swear to tell me nothing but the truth in the name of the Lord?"* Then Micaiah gave the true word from the Lord. *"I saw all Israel scattered on the hills like sheep without a shepherd, and the Lord said, 'These people have no master. Let each one go home in peace.'"* Ahab said to Jehoshaphat, *"Did not I tell you that he never prophesies anything good about me, but only bad?"* Micaiah continued with the word of the Lord, including what God showed him about the prophets being deceived by a lying spirit. It did not go well for this prophet. He was slapped by one of the false prophets and ordered by the king to be thrown in jail with only bread and water. The events unfolded just as the true prophet said, and Ahab died in battle.

Now back to the present day. Most Christians only want to hear what will edify, comfort, and encourage them. That is the *gift* of prophecy, which any Christian is able to operate in. It truly is God's desire for every believer to be edified, comforted, and encouraged.

However, the prophet will see what God sees and say what God is saying, and there are times that the recipient of the ministry is not necessarily thinking he is being comforted or encouraged at the time.

It will bring change if we respond to their words. We are not to fear or try to control what they say.

Let me share a personal story. Many years ago, my husband and I received prophetic ministry. We were given some very encouraging words, and they were surely from the Lord because of how specific the prophecy was. This prophetic ministry edified, comforted, and encouraged us just as the *gift* of prophecy is supposed to do. At the end, a *seasoned* prophet who was overseeing the ministry being given to us said that the Lord showed him something about me.

He said, "I see the Lord working in some areas, particularly in the area of control." (I must say here I was immediately offended at God for saying that *in front* of my husband!) He went on to say, among other things, "God is going to challenge you in that area and start taking you down a road where He is going to see if you really trust Him and really are able to accept what happens to you and in your family as God's perfect will... It is a major area that God wants to break, and the enemy is trying to use that even to bring division in the marriage. You guys are on the verge of moving into your destiny, and it is just a place that God has brought to the surface now, and as you relinquish that control and give control back to the Lord then you free Him up to move. Those things that seem to be in concrete that you are praying for will be released, and you will see the miracle-working hand of God."

I did not speak to God for several days. However, when I typed out the prophecy that week, I saw the part about being on the verge of moving into destiny and that it was the enemy's work causing me to operate in fear and mistrust of God. I got back on speaking terms with the Lord (smile). If the prophetic ministry to us had only been to edify, comfort, and encourage us, I would still be stuck where I was. As it turns out, even after realizing a problem had been identified, it still took several years to let go of the control in *every* area of my life. Had I not been told the truth at that time, I would have thought I was waiting on God to move, instead of Him waiting on me to *change*. The ministry of the prophet is desperately needed.

2

WHAT IS THE DIFFERENCE BETWEEN THE PSYCHIC AND THE PROPHETIC?

When I was in my twenties, someone I worked with told me about her experience with a fortune teller and how accurate the person was. She told me that it only cost $5.00. Since I believed in the supernatural, it was not long before I was going monthly to the fortune teller. She told me things that were true. "Your boyfriend's name starts with an 'M.' His name is something like 'Mike.' He works on the water and lives on the water." I was dating Mike Anderson, who is now my husband. His office was on the end of the City Marina with a view of the water, and he lived in an apartment overlooking the bay. This correct information served to "hook" me, and the lady was very nice. She had an open Bible on the dresser, and she told my fortune with a deck of cards. She truly believed this was a gift from God that she was employing.

The last time I visited the fortune teller for a "reading," she said to me, "This is your last time to come here." I said "No, I will be back." Within a month, I gave my life to the Lord. A while later, I saw her in the lobby of a movie theater and she said to me, "I *told* you that you were not coming back."

After becoming a believer, I did not go back to see the fortune teller. Around four years later, I encountered the true prophetic gift. A Jewish man from New Zealand, full of the Holy Spirit, was the guest speaker at the church I attended. The power of God was displayed as people were healed immediately, accurate words of knowledge were given, and prophetic words about the future came forth. Since that time, God has unraveled all my wrong beliefs and the mixture that was in my mind about the source of knowledge and whether fortune tellers could really tell the future. As it turns out, there is proof that they *cannot* tell the future. They would be the wealthy people on the earth. They would know what to invest in on the stock market. They would know the winning lottery tickets' numbers. Criminals would have them on staff.

What is the difference between the psychic and the prophetic? The primary difference is the source. To further clarify, *source* is defined as a place, person, or thing from which something originates. Where is the information given by prophetic people or psychics originating? *Webster's 1828 American Dictionary* defines prophecy as, "A foretelling; prediction; a declaration of something to come. As God only knows future events with certainty, no being but God or some person *informed by [H]im,* can utter a real prophecy."

I am God, and there is no other; I am God, and there is none like me. I make known the end from the beginning, from ancient times, what is still to come. I say: My purpose will stand, and I will do all that I please. (Isaiah 46:9b-10) Notice that in this verse God says He makes the end known and what is still to come. Only God has this power.

So, how does the psychic get his information? How does it work that true things are spoken? The answer is that there is a network in the spirit realm. When I went to the fortune teller, the spirit that was giving her information was communicating with spirits that were around me and was given details that were already revealed in my life. Anyone around me could tell her that my boyfriend's name was Mike and where he worked and lived. These were not mysteries that only God could know. After the woman told me facts, however, I believed the other things that she told me. It could be that the other things would be the direction the enemy of my soul would have me go.

Prophecy has its source in God. The Lord will speak through a person, often addressing things from the past, then the present, then the future. He will, through prophetic words, call things that are *not* as if they were. He speaks to things that have not happened and calls them into existence. There is power in true prophecy. *[...] God who gives life to the dead and calls things that are not as though they were. And this promise is from God Himself, who makes the dead live again and speaks of future events with as much certainty as though they were already past.* (Romans 4:17b LB)

So, the bottom line is this. The gift that is the true prophetic gift does not rely on information that is already given, as does the demonic counterfeit. It is a communiqué from the living God. The demonic counterfeit is giving information gathered by the demonic network. For instance, a fortune teller or psychic could tell a business man, "I see a contract." Let us just say that day he bid on the contract. The psychic would go on to say, "You are being awarded a large contract." The truth behind the scenes is that the bids were opened, and it is written down that this man was the low bidder. That is *revealed* information. That is not telling the future even though the next day he may get a phone call saying he was the low bidder. Demonic spirits communicated revealed knowledge.

The true prophetic gift always directs people to God.

Here is a Biblical example of a king who needed to find out what a disturbing dream meant. *The king asked Daniel (also called Belteshazzar), "Are you able to tell me what I saw in my dream and interpret it?" Daniel replied, "No wise man, enchanter, magician or diviner can explain to the king the mystery he has asked about, but **there is a God in heaven who reveals mysteries.**"* (Daniel 2:26-28)

Here is what the Scriptures have to say regarding getting spiritual help.

> When you enter the land the Lord your God is giving you, do not learn to imitate the detestable ways of the nations there. Let no one be found among you who sacrifices his son or daughter in the fire, who practices divination or sorcery, interprets omens, engages in witchcraft, or casts spells, or who is a medium or **spiritist** or who consults the dead. Anyone who does these things is detestable to the Lord, and because of these detestable practices the Lord your God will drive out those nations before you. You must be blameless before the Lord your God. The nations you will dispossess listen to those who practice sorcery or divination. But as for you, the Lord your God has not permitted you to do so. **The Lord your God will raise up for you a prophet** like me from among your own brothers. You must listen to him. (Deuteronomy 18:9-15)

God calls these things detestable and abominations, and says that His people need to listen to His prophets, not the enemy's counterfeits.

The disciples encountered a girl with a spirit of divination who was telling fortunes.

Once when we were going to the place of prayer, we were met by a slave girl who had a spirit by which she predicted the future. She earned a great deal of money for her owners by fortune-telling. This girl followed Paul and the rest of us, shouting, "These men are servants of the Most High God, who are telling you the way to be saved." She kept this up for many days. Finally Paul became so troubled that he turned around and said to the spirit, "In the name of Jesus Christ I command you to come out of her!" At that moment the spirit left her. (Acts 16:16-18)

It was obvious that they were servants of God and were telling the people how to be saved. It did not take a supernatural gift to make that statement. Something about this annoyed Paul, and after a few days of praying about this, Paul got disturbed and provoked enough to cast out the spirit. Without the demonic spirit, she could not tell fortunes anymore.

Are People Born with the Gift to be Psychic or Prophetic?

There are people who are born with the gift of being very sensitive spiritually. They hear things, see things, and know things that other people are not hearing, seeing, and knowing. This happens to Christians and non-Christians. Most gifts that people receive from God are given at birth. For instance, a person may be gifted musically or vocally, and that gift can be used for good or evil. The anointing can draw people to the Lord, or they can use that anointing to draw people into darkness by the lyrics they sing or music they play.

When I was young, I played a game. I would say, "Turn on the radio, I bet I can tell you what song is playing right now." Then we would click on the car radio and most of the time I was right. As a young adult, I was driving down the road and a sign was being painted and I *knew* somehow what would be painted on the sign.

I was very sensitive and could read people's feelings. Sometimes when I entered a department store, I could tell that the salesperson did not trust me and felt that I was going to steal something. I was careful to keep my hands and movements out in the open so as to prove to them I was *not* a criminal!

The Lord showed me recently that most people withhold love to show displeasure and to discipline. Because of being very sensitive spiritually all my life, discerning this "withholding of love" made me feel as a child that I was being rejected for who I was. This caused me to try to please everyone because I hated the feeling of rejection. Even though I was born to be a leader, I became a follower and did things against my conscience so that I would not be rejected.

I have shared all that to show that as an unbeliever the prophetic gift was working in my life. I was dedicated to the Lord as a baby. Although I wandered quite a bit, I finally gave my life to the Lord at age 25. The enemy did not get to turn my gift to the psychic realm. There are people, however, who realized they had a gift and unknowingly began to tap into the enemy's source. That is why, today, we can ask a person in the New Age or occult, and they will tell us with certainty that their gift is God-given.

If you have been involved with psychics in any way, or are not sure of the source of information you have tapped into, or if you or your ancestors have been involved in other occult practices, you need to repent and get free from these evil influences.

You could pray this prayer:

Lord, I repent for my sins and those of my ancestors for every occult practice we have been involved in. (If you know what they are, name them individually.) I renounce every source of power and information that is not holy and does not originate with You. Lord, I would rather not have any power or gifting unless it comes from You. I command any evil spirits that have operated through me to be gone in Jesus name. Amen.

When we consecrate ourselves to the Lord, and renounce any power or source that is not God, we can be used by the Lord.

3

WHAT IS THE PURPOSE OF THE FIVE-FOLD MINISTRY?

It was He [God] who gave some to be apostles, some to be prophets, some to be evangelists, and some to be pastors and teachers, **to prepare God's people for works of service,** so that the body of Christ may be built up until we all reach unity in the faith and in the knowledge of the Son of God and become mature, attaining to the whole measure of the fullness of Christ until we all reach unity in the faith and in the knowledge of the Son of God and become mature, attaining to the whole measure of the fullness of Christ. (Ephesians 4:11-13)

One day it became clear to me about the purpose of the five-fold ministry. Most Christians I knew perceived it incorrectly. We were not familiar with the above Scriptures. Somehow, we became over-dependent on leaders and expected *them* to do all the "works of service" or "the work of the ministry." We felt totally unprepared to be used by God ourselves, which kept us from exercising faith and positioning ourselves to be active in the kingdom of God. In our minds, our religious duty was to attend church regularly and pray.

This mindset kept us in a "someone else is responsible to 'feed me'" mode. We were looking for another teaching, another prophetic word, or another instruction. God's intention was to have the leaders He placed over us to teach us the basics. They were to teach us *the elementary teachings of Jesus Christ.* These teachings are listed in Hebrews 6:1-2, *repentance from dead works and of faith toward God, the doctrine of baptisms, of laying on of hands, of resurrection of the dead, and of eternal judgment.* It also stated we were to go on to maturity.

I now realize that these leaders were to teach us how to hear God in the many ways He speaks to us. We needed to be instructed how to pursue an intimate relationship with God, and to learn the fear of the Lord. Teachers did not know we needed to be taught how to find instruction in the Word of God for ourselves. Pastors should have been truthful about error and authority and true connection with the Body of Christ. We needed them to love us enough to tell us the truth. They were to help identify our gifts and callings, train us where we needed training and encourage us to step out with what we knew. These leaders were to prepare *us* to do the work of the ministry. Of course, with our wrong mindset, we expected *them* to do the work of the ministry. Our real need was to know how to be a real person and reach people with the simplicity of the Gospel message. This wrong perspective is why we have had such fruitless lives. I personally sat back feeling like I was not ready and became so wrapped up in myself that I touched no one else along the way.

Good news! Things are changing! God is restoring His order to the Church by bringing apostolic order. Apostles are new as far as our experience goes, but we must openly embrace what the Lord is doing. Remember, *It was He* [God] *who gave some to be* **apostles**. As the five-fold ministry does what it was intended to do, the Church is arising.

A Little More Clarity

How can we tell if those in the five-fold ministry are doing their part? It is not just whether they have been trained and prepared in the eyes of man. A fruitful five-fold minister equips the people to do ministry themselves.

We must remember that those who "have turned the world upside down" in Acts 17:6 were unlearned. *Now when they saw the boldness of Peter and John, and perceived that they were unlearned and ignorant men, they marveled; and they took knowledge of them, that* **they had been with Jesus**. (Acts 4:13) Ministers today need to have this mark on them. Is it obvious that they have been with Jesus? This was stated about Peter and John after the lame man at the Beautiful Gate had been **healed** and they had **preached** to the crowd that gathered.

4

WHAT IS PROPHECY?

Prophecy is a prediction or the foretelling of what is to come in the future. Most of the time another gift of the Spirit works along with prophecy. An example would be the "word of knowledge." The Lord may identify something from the past or present that lets us know He really knows us. I personally believe this builds our faith to receive what He wants to tell us about the future through the prophetic word.

A common misconception about prophecy is: "If God said it, it will come to pass *no matter what.*" We must understand that the majority of prophetic words are conditional and require some kind of response from us. What I mean by being conditional is if I do my part and meet the conditions, God will do His part.

The Lord uses prophetic ministry to reveal, by the way of an invitation, what He has in store for us.

There is a scriptural basis for this. We need to understand God's Word and His ways. Take this verse for instance: *For God so loved the world that He gave His one and only Son, that whoever believes in Him shall not perish but have eternal life.* (John 3:16) It is prophetically stated here in this verse that *whoever believes in Him* will be saved. His will is expressed, and it is up to the individual. So it is with prophecy. He expresses what He wants to take place through the prophetic word, and it is up to the person to cooperate with Him in order for it to come to pass. For instance, many years ago, I was told that one day I would write a book. If I had never sat down with a pen and paper or at a computer and begun to write, it would never have happened. If I had not exercised my faith and taken action, it would still be a prophetic word and the fault would be mine, not God's. I could not call a person a false prophet because the prophetic word had not come to pass.

I have heard people judge the person who gave them a prophetic word because it had not come to pass. We need to know that during the time that passes, the Lord is working on our character. He is not looking at a clock to see if it is time for the fulfillment. He is looking for the change to take place in us.

Prophetic words are not automatic, and there are some things we are even going to have to fight for. Paul said *Timothy, my son, I give you this instruction in keeping with the prophecies once made about you, so that by following them you may fight the good fight, holding on to faith and a good conscience. Some have rejected these and so have shipwrecked their faith.* (1 Timothy 1:18-19) In the New King James version, it says, *This charge I commit to you, son Timothy, according to the prophecies previously made concerning you, that by them you may* **wage the good warfare** (v. 18).

How is the warfare waged? We must stand in faith and agree with God, yielding to what He wants to change in us, and most importantly continue to walk with Him in obedience. We are progressively being conformed into the image of Jesus Christ, and the Holy Spirit is determined to complete that work. We can fulfill our destiny, and God will get the greatest glory as we die to our carnal nature and are changed. Strongholds in our lives prevent our growth, and our willingness to deal with issues takes time, too. As time passes and we let God change us, we become the people of character that can fit the prophetic word.

No, it isn't your imagination –
God measures time differently from us.

When, in a prophetic word, God says to you "this night" or "from this day forth," it means something has been released in the spirit realm and it will take place in your life but... remember a day as is a thousand years with the Lord (smile). It could still be a while before it comes to pass. When He uses the word "soon," it could be sometime in the next few years.

5

JUDGING PROPHECY: DOES PROPHECY ALWAYS CONFIRM WHAT GOD HAS PREVIOUSLY SHOWN ME IN MY HEART?

Because of the abuse of the "prophetic," there are many people who are skeptical or who have even rejected this particular gift of the Holy Spirit. It is commonly stated that a way to judge prophecy is that it will *always* confirm what God has previously spoken to a person in his or her own heart. Many times, this is the case. But, there are also times that what is spoken prophetically has never even crossed our mind!

Let me share some Biblical examples of this.

- There is no record of David knowing that he would be the King of Israel prior to him being called from the shepherd's field by the prophet Samuel, after his brothers were passed over (1 Samuel 16).

- Israel did not believe the prophecies given to them by Jeremiah that they would be taken into exile in Babylon (Jeremiah 19 and 20). There are many times the words of the prophets were rejected, resulting in their persecution and sometimes death.

- Since God is able to do exceedingly, abundantly above what we can dare ask or think, there are times that He will expand our vision through prophecy and say things confirming something we already thought or that He had spoken to our heart. There are times that God will call us something we *know* we are not. Gideon, for example, was called a mighty man of war. At the time, he was threshing wheat in a wine press to hide it from the enemy. The angel of the Lord came and talked to him (Judges 6:11). Gideon was told that he would save Israel from the Midianites. Apparently, it never occurred to him prior to this encounter because he even tried to explain why he couldn't do it.

- When Elisha the prophet told the woman she would have a baby by that same time next year, she accused him of lying to her (2 Kings 4:16).

Nuggets:

- God uses prophecy to steer our life and give us vision.

- The "Word of the Lord" will test us, which means it will seem as if the prophetic word will never come to pass. During this time, it is like we are being *sifted as wheat* to have the motives of our heart exposed in order that we will grow and change. A biblical example of this is Joseph. He had a prophetic dream concerning his family bowing down to him. Seventeen years later it came to pass. In the meantime, he was kidnapped and rejected by his brothers, thrown into a pit, sold into slavery, falsely accused, thrown into prison, and *then* raised up second-in-command under Pharaoh. The day came that his family bowed down to him, not knowing who he was. His story is retold by the Psalmist, and it says, *Until the time that his word came to pass, the word of the Lord tested him.* (Psalm 105:19 NKJ)

- A ministry call on a person's life may be a surprise to him or her. This is particularly true of those with low self-esteem because they have been convinced that God could never use them.

6

HOW TO RESPOND TO PERSONAL PROPHECY

All personal prophecy should be recorded for the benefit of the person receiving it so he or she can have an accurate record of what was said. It also protects the minister who gives it because not everyone's memory is good, and it prevents misunderstandings.

When you receive a personal prophecy, you should:

- Write or type out the prophetic word.

- Review the prophecy with your spiritual covering (pastor/elder/mentor).

Keep these things in mind:

- Prophecies are not self-fulfilling. They will require cooperation on your part. Faith and obedience are the keys.

- Between the time the prophecy is given and its fulfillment, God is working on your character.

- It is quite normal for the prophecy to bring you into a time of testing.

- Do not take action based on a word without receiving confirmation and counsel.

7

HEARING THE VOICE OF GOD

My sheep hear My voice, and I know them, and they follow
Me. (John 10:27 NKJ)

My sister moved from the hectic metropolis of Atlanta to the
countryside of Arkansas. She then decided that she wanted to raise
some sheep. When she acquired them, she named each one whatever
they reminded her of. One was named "Marilyn," after Marilyn
Monroe. Another was named "Charlie," after my mother's late
husband, and on it went from there. I eventually made the long drive
out to Arkansas to visit her.

She was showing me around the farm and said, "Let me show you
something." She said, "Call the sheep."

I had zero experience with animals and managed to call out, "Here, sheep. Here, sheep!" and the sheep with heads down, kept grazing on the other side of the fence.

Then she said, "Marilyn!" Up popped the head of one of the sheep, and it looked directly at her. "Charlie!" Instantly another sheep looked at her. The sheep knew her voice, and she called them all by name. That was a cool moment.

I stood there and watched a Scripture come alive.

> The watchman opens the gate for him, and the sheep listen to his voice. He calls his own sheep by name and leads them out. When he has brought out all his own, he goes on ahead of them, and his sheep follow him because they know his voice. But they will never follow a stranger [...] because they do not recognize a stranger's voice. (John 10:3-5)

The Lord desires a good connection with His people. We cannot connect without communication. It is vital in any healthy relationship.

Three things greatly hinder this:

- Ignorance: Not knowing how much God desires to communicate is one thing.

- Unbelief: Not believing He wants to communicate with us personally is another.

- Apathy: Not caring enough to pursue it is the worst.

Two-way communication with the God of the universe is a wonderful privilege, and He desires to have it with each of us. The Holy Spirit will lead and teach us in the art of hearing God.

Following is one of my lessons:

Years ago, I left the smaller children at home with my two teenagers and went to do my weekly grocery shopping. About 30 minutes later, I was pushing my overflowing cart around the grocery store, and heard in my thoughts, "Go home! Something is wrong!" This was alarming to me, and my thoughts went wild. Now this was before cell phones, and I did not have change for a payphone, so I had a decision to make. Was this God talking to me? I heard it again, "Go home! Something is wrong!" I felt a lot of pressure to go and find out what was wrong.

It came to my mind that there was a verse that said to test the spirits.

Dear friends, do not believe every spirit, but test the spirits to see whether they are from God [...]. This is how you can recognize the Spirit of God: Every spirit that acknowledges that Jesus Christ has come in the flesh is from God, but every spirit that does not acknowledge Jesus is not from God. (1 John 4:1-3)

Then I spoke in a very low, discreet manner, "You, spirit that is speaking to me, do you confess that Jesus Christ has come in the flesh?" I heard total silence. It was not God talking to me. I found out that God does not get offended if we want to be sure it is His voice before acting on something. I had total peace and continued my shopping.

There were other times that I *thought* God was telling me to do something and acted on it, and it did not turn out to be Him. Hearing the voice of the Lord is something we grow in. We learn to recognize His voice. I found out that the Lord does not push us, or talk demeaning or in an angry tone. He is much kinder to me than I am to myself.

God is much more willing to talk to us than we are willing to take the time to be still and listen to Him. The difficulty is not with Him, it is with us. It takes faith to hear Him.

Here is another one of my lessons: I had already cleaned the kitchen and put the leftovers from dinner in the refrigerator. *Hmmmmm, maybe I need just a little bit more pecan pie*, I thought to myself. (I see you smiling.) I opened the refrigerator door and was reaching for it when

I had a thought that I did not need more pie. I shrugged it off, put the pie on the counter, and was reaching for a knife when I heard in my spirit, "How can you say you hear My voice when you cannot hear Me say you do not need more pie?" Uh-oh! Yes, it is the little things that we need to pay attention to, if we expect to hear greater things.

> May the God of peace, who through the blood of the eternal covenant brought back from the dead our Lord Jesus, that **great Shepherd of the sheep**, equip you with everything good for doing His will, and may He work in us what is pleasing to Him, through Jesus Christ, to whom be glory for ever and ever. Amen. (Hebrews 13:20-21)

Here is a prayer you could pray:

> *Lord, I repent for ignoring many times what You were communicating to me. I want to grow in my ability to hear Your voice and to obediently listen. Teach me and continue to lead me in the truth. In Jesus name. Amen.*

8

THE IMPORTANCE OF HUMILITY

All of you, clothe yourselves with humility toward one another, because, "God opposes the proud but gives grace to the humble." Humble yourselves, therefore, under God's mighty hand, that He may lift you up in due time. (1 Peter 5:5b-6)

One of the greatest lessons I have learned is how God feels about pride versus humility. He went to a great deal of trouble to teach me. What caused me to learn humility? Ordinary circumstances revealed quite a bit *about* me *to* me. Once I realized what God was after in the circumstances He permitted in my life, I was able to laugh at myself and embrace the humbling process. The above verse says *God opposes the proud*. I do not want God opposing me!

Let me share one of my "humbling" stories. When my youngest son, Jonathan, was six weeks old, I took him and Christopher, who was four, to the beach to visit a friend of mine. We walked down to the beach. I carried a lightweight baby bassinette with a net over it because the yellow flies were biting. Christopher was burying my legs in the sand, which I did not mind since it would prevent bites. I relaxed at the beach, and my husband drove out that night and joined us for a wonderful Italian dinner with our friends.

During the night, I started itching badly on my legs and I presumed it was from the bites. The next day, the itching grew worse. That night, it was so bad that I had to get up and put ice on the places to numb them. Then, I had no choice but to go to a dermatologist to find out what was going on. He took one look at my legs and said, "You have worms." Apparently a cat had pooped in the sand, and the parasites had got into the skin on my legs and also Christopher's hands. The cure for the worms was for us to take a cherry flavored medicine that would kill them. I could not take the medicine orally because I was nursing the baby, and it would have passed through the milk to him. So, I had to put it on my legs twice a day (very sticky and sweet smelling) and wrap my legs with Saran Wrap® so it would absorb. This is hilarious to me now, and I knew it had to have a divine purpose. During this time, I was at a Christian leadership meeting, and as we were sitting there, I crossed my legs and everyone could hear the crinkling sound of Saran Wrap® even though it was hidden by my slacks.

I said to a few people after telling my story, "Maybe the Lord is trying to teach me something."

Someone replied, "God would *never* use something like this to teach you something." Down inside my "knower," I knew better. And I realized although God did not cause me to get worms in my legs, He could surely use it to deal with the pride issue in my life. Since pride seems to die in increments, this had a measure of success.

A Few Quotes from God's Word

You save the humble but bring low those whose eyes are haughty. (Psalm 18:27)

The arrogance of man will be brought low and the pride of men humbled; the Lord alone will be exalted in that day. (Isaiah 2:17)

He guides the humble in what is right and teaches them His way. (Psalm 25:9)

For the Lord takes delight in His people; He crowns the humble with salvation. (Psalm 149:4)

He mocks proud mockers but gives grace to the humble. (Proverbs 3:34)

Let me tell you another story about how God broke some pride in my life. Years ago, I was going to an international Aglow Conference in Washington, D.C. At that time, it seemed that all I did was "pump up" Christians and try to convince them not to give up.

I was in prayer prior to the trip, and said to the Lord, "It seems that there are not many 'believers' who *believe*." I came across a verse where the Apostle Paul was saying to the church in Rome that he longed to come to see them *that you and I may be mutually encouraged by each other's faith.* (Romans 1:12) It brought tears to my eyes, and I prayed that the Lord would give me an opportunity on this trip to talk to someone who encouraged me, too. It turned out that God provided a time with an acquaintance from Tallahassee, and we were both encouraged by each other's testimony of God's faithfulness. However, something happened to me on the trip. I went from being the person who wept when I came across the verse mentioned above, to a place where I judged people for not believing. (Pride always judges others.) On the last morning, I could not even enter into the worship and did not know why. I asked the Lord what was wrong with me.

He said, "Pride."

I said, "You will have to humble me, I do not even know how to humble myself." Then I forgot all about it as the conference ended and we all began gathering our things to travel home.

It was wintertime, and we had traveled on two planes to get to the conference. We had carried our coats and placed them in the overhead compartments. Now it was the trip home. I entered my plane along with ten smiling, glowing ladies. We were quite an attraction! I reached for the overhead compartment to put my coat in, just like I had done on the trip a few days before. I read the words "EMERGENCY ONLY – LIFE RAFT," but the words did not register quickly enough, and I pulled the lever. A compartment opened that was over six feet long. (Thank goodness, it did not inflate!)

The stewardess walked up to me and said, *"Can't* you read?"

Everybody was laughing, and so I joined in, too, while inside I was wishing I was dead and wondering how God could *ever* use someone as dumb as me. Little tears were in the corner of my eyes, and I exercised much restraint to keep from bawling. Pride was assaulted once again. Remember, it dies little by little. It turned out that I was able to witness to and pray with the guy next to me on the plane after this happened and my ego was down to size.

Pride goes before destruction, a haughty spirit before a fall. (Proverbs 16:18)

For whoever exalts himself will be humbled, and whoever humbles himself will be exalted. (Matthew 23:12)

You must learn humility,
and God will help you. (smile)

9

WOUNDED PROPHETIC PEOPLE

Becoming a humble person, yielded to God, can be a painful process. As prophetic people we are often overlooked (God's strategy to cause us to realize we are not as awesome as we think). At times, He makes us invisible to those in ministry around us. We are recognized only as someone who can do something that a servant would do. Hold the door, carry the box, keep the children, etc.

There is a great price to pay to be God's mouthpiece. You may say to yourself, "I did not ask for this. I never wanted to be a prophet!" I have said those words, too. But, the intimacy that is available for those who will get close enough to God to hear His heart makes it worth it all.

I know what it is like to be troubled by what I see going on in the Body of Christ. I know what it is like to feel like I have something to say and there is no one who wants to hear it. I know what it is like to see what is wrong, but be powerless to say anything and be heard. This is where an intercessor is born. There is something you can say and there is something you can do. You can pray. Not all intercessors are prophets, but all prophets are intercessors. There is much pent-up frustration in those who see, and then do nothing with what they see. It is possible to move to a different church. However, it will not be long before you see what is wrong in that church, too.

Another problem is that the one who "sees" does not understand why everyone else does not see it, too. It is so obvious! The Scriptures say that there are many members in the Body of Christ. The eyes and the ears are individual parts of the body. The other parts do not see and hear what the eyes and ears are finding out. The Bible also says there are the unseemly parts and those parts are hidden. Prayer is a hidden work. This is based on 1 Corinthians 12.

Because of all the misunderstanding, rejection, and humbling a prophetic person must go through to be a spokesman for the Lord, there is healing that must take place along the way. Let me share an illustration. When my children were small, they really liked Kool-Aid®. However, I found that if I mixed Kool-Aid® in a plastic pitcher, the flavor absorbed into the plastic. Then when I made tea in the same pitcher, it tainted the flavor of the tea. This is what it is like to try to be God's messenger when we are wounded. If there are hurts, unforgiveness, judging, and other unresolved issues, the message we attempt to deliver for the Lord becomes tainted by what is in us. We can think we are interpreting the Lord's feelings when, in fact, they are our own. Many people have been helped by using my book *Rising from Defeat* to deal with the issues in their lives. I also highly recommend *A Tale of Three Kings* by Gene Edwards. It is a study in brokenness. It is time to get healed.

Pain and misunderstanding come with the prophetic call because you are different. But much suffering can be avoided by asking for wisdom and applying it.

10

THE CALL OF A PROPHET

Many years ago, I felt the call of a prophet on my life. I thought that possibly it was my imagination. Smith Wigglesworth's stories made quite an impression on me, and I began to have thoughts of me doing "acts of power." By acts of power I mean because of my prayers and obedience to the Lord, the miraculous would take place – like people on their death bed being raised up. I was also drawn over and over to the book of Jeremiah. The verses that spoke to me were:

> The word of the Lord came to me, saying, "Before I formed you in the womb I knew you, before you were born I set you apart; I appointed you as a prophet to the nations." "Ah, Sovereign Lord," I said, "I do not know how to speak; I am only a child." But the Lord said to me, "Do not say, 'I am only a child.' You must go to everyone I send you to and say whatever I command you. Do not be afraid of them, for I am with you and will rescue you," declares the

Lord. Then the Lord reached out His hand and touched my mouth and said to me, "Now, I have put My words in your mouth." (Jeremiah 1:4-9)

In 1984, I was called forward at the ministry time by an Aglow retreat speaker. She reached out and touched my lips and said, "Your lips are anointed. The Lord would say unto you, My hand is mightily upon you and I will use you in the way that I have spoken to your heart that I would use you, says the Lord. That was not your imagination. That was Me that spoke that to your heart and you have yet to see it come to pass, but know that I am grooming you for that day and that hour when you will proclaim My Word in might and power, says the Lord. I anoint your lips. Say not that I am but a youth, but you will go to whom I tell you and you will speak the words that I tell you and they will bring praise and worship to My name." This was the first confirmation I received concerning the call of a prophet.

About that time, I had a prophetic dream. In the dream, I was in the lobby of a building the size of the Empire State Building. There were many people standing there besides myself. They said that someone was being chosen to go to the top. I was looking left and right to see who they chose to go up. Then, they walked right up to me. I knew I was no different from the rest and felt so honored and excited. The elevator opened. I walked in, and the elevator operator took me to the top. The doors opened. I stepped out and, to my surprise, there was nothing there. It was only a ramp going down and it was as wide as a skating rink. There was no one in sight. I began to walk down the steep incline very carefully, so I would not slide. After a while, I thought it was the end, but I turned the corner, and it kept going down. This happened several times before I got the idea to "snow plow." (The "snow plow" is a technique for snow skiing that is taught to beginners. It is how to control the speed of downward skiing by forming a wedge with your skis.) I used this technique in my dream and sped up the final stretch. I was so excited to have finally made it to the bottom. I looked to the right side, and there was a small bleacher set up with some of the most humble people I have ever seen. Even their clothing was such that they did not stand out from each other. There was a microphone set up on a stand in front of the bleachers. I walked up to the microphone to announce that I had finally made it to the bottom. I awakened my husband laughing with joy!

The Lord showed me that this was the call of the prophet. The higher the calling, the greater the walk of humility that would be required. Down, down, down I would go in my eyes and in the eyes of man. By cooperating with God, the final part of the process would speed up. Someone once said, "It takes a *lot* of humiliation to produce a *little* humility." And yes, the process was greatly humiliating. There is joy in the end, however.

In the beginning, I began to see with God's perspective some things about the condition of the Body of Christ. But, having much more zeal than wisdom, I did not know what to do with what I saw. Little did I realize that what I was seeing was for intercession and not to be told. It seems that budding prophets think they are like the prophets of old, so most of the prophetic insight they speak has a degree of judgment in it. That leads some to take on a martyr spirit and think that they are being persecuted for Christ's sake when what they spoke was not received. Immaturity and a lack of having been mentored are reasons for this. Part of this process served as humiliation and helped to prepare me to become a prophet of the present day. There is more than prophesying in the prophetic office. The main focus of a prophet must be intercession. There were those who helped to mentor me, but more attention was given to developing the prophetic gift than on character-building and dying to self.

How I tried to fulfill my destiny! Knowing what the Lord had spoken to me personally, along with the prophetic words that came through strangers in the Body of Christ, I knew there was a call on my life. I did everything in my power to cooperate and even "help" the Lord (smile). Our fleshly efforts cannot fulfill the will and purposes of God. It can only mess up what is of divine origin. Because our destiny comes from the Lord, our time with Him is the greatest preparation.

Our time in His Word is our revelation of Him and even our revelation of ourselves. The revelation of ourselves is seeing how our hearts need to be changed and our motives purified.

We work with Him as we pray for these changes and they take place. Our minds are renewed to know Him as He really is.

> "Let him who boasts, boast about this: that he understands and knows Me, that I am the Lord, who exercises kindness, justice and righteousness on earth, for in these I delight," declares the Lord. (Jeremiah 9:24)

11

MATURING IN THE PROPHETIC

There are several important keys to maturing in the prophetic gifting:

- Study the Scriptures.

- Exercise the gift.

- Be mentored – both through anointed teaching in books, videos, and recordings and under a prophetic mentor. (See recommended reading in the back of the book.)

As a prophetic person, the most important relationship we need to develop and maintain is with the Lord. We must fight for it. We will not just stumble into this relationship. It must be pursued diligently.

Regarding the need to mature, following is my observation of a prophetic intercessor who was a budding prophet. I was at a conference, and someone who was a very strong prayer leader and had a position in the ministry gave a prophetic word. What she did bothered me because I have a strong gift of discernment. She seemed frustrated and upset. There was nothing wrong with her words, but it was the spirit in which the message was delivered. A little later in the day, the conversation I had with the Lord really helped me.

I asked the Lord a couple of questions. *Is this You that is so upset with our immaturity? Was this You in the message that was given, warning people, or was it her interpretation of how she thought You felt? Was it in her time with You that she got the message that she gave? Hmmmm... maybe she is not spending enough time with You to see how You feel.*

The Lord said to me: *I [God] am not upset. When, from a human standpoint, one sees the condition (and what she sees is accurate), one can become very frustrated with what one sees. But I [God] am not frustrated. So, yes, what she sees is accurate, but her response is not My response. Pray for her to mature in this area. She needs to mature in My love. For she has taken up My cause and fights for Me. It is not necessary for her to fight for Me. I am a Big God. She was perceiving the truth with a false burden. Which made her feel compelled to give a prophetic word. Prayer was the proper course for her to take. As you perceived, it was not profitable. No one received what she said.*

I realized from this conversation with the Lord that when someone gives a prophetic word, he is speaking *for* God. The message is to communicate what God is saying and how He feels. There are some things that we see or know because we have the prophetic gifting. What we do with these things is another story.

Getting Free Enough to be Used by the Lord

People are born with motivational gifts and they have an invitation by God to mature and be used in those gifts.

Areas to mature in:

- I must overcome all that would hinder me from obeying.

- He wants all of my heart.

- I must be changed to fit the call of God on my life. How am I in the areas of integrity, faithfulness, forgiveness, humility, etc.?

I have heard it said that God uses those who are *available*. Over the years, many people in public ministry fell into disgrace through unrepented sin. After the Charismatic movement, I heard a strong prophetic person say that in the next move, God would only use *clean* vessels. The Lord is no longer satisfied that we are just available; we must be cleansed and prepared. This is taking place now.

There is a prophetic word that John the Baptist proclaimed concerning Jesus and the cleansing He would do:

> I baptize you with water for repentance. But after me will come one who is more powerful than I, whose sandals I am not fit to carry. He will baptize you with the Holy Spirit and with fire. His winnowing fork is in His hand, and He will clear His threshing floor, gathering His wheat into the barn and burning up the chaff with unquenchable fire. (Matthew 3:11-12)

Keep in mind that the chaff is the husk of the grain. It served its purpose in housing the grain, but is useless after harvest.

12

WHAT JESUS TAUGHT CONCERNING PROPHETS

The people that Jesus taught already knew that there were true prophets. In Matthew 5, He taught what is commonly referred to as the Beatitudes and He said, *Blessed are you when people insult you, persecute you and falsely say all kinds of evil against you because of Me. Rejoice and be glad, because great is your reward in heaven, for in the same way they persecuted the **prophets** who were before you.* In the course of His teaching, He referred to the prophets Daniel, Isaiah, and Jonah, and the foundation of the Law and the Prophets.

He taught that there was a true benefit to receive from a prophet and his ministry. *Anyone who receives a prophet because he is a prophet will receive a prophet's reward, and anyone who receives a righteous man because he is a righteous man will receive a righteous man's reward. And if anyone gives even a cup of cold water to one of these little ones because he is My disciple, I tell you the truth, he will certainly not lose his reward.* (Matthew 10:41-42) The word "reward" is used three times here. Merriam-Webster's Dictionary gives the definition of reward as "something that is given in return for good or evil done or received and especially that is offered or given for some service or attainment."

The Lord desires that His people recognize and receive from one another the gifting and the contribution that each has. Our reward comes from embracing and receiving that gift. It is implied that if we do not receive a prophet or a righteous man (a person who is in right relationship with God), or one of the little ones because he is His disciple, we literally miss receiving what that person has to contribute to the Body of Christ.

Having laid the groundwork of how Jesus viewed prophets, we will look at a warning He gave. There is much to be gained by breaking down Jesus' teaching in Matthew 7 (NKJ), so I will do it verse by verse.

V. 15 *Beware* [be cautious and alert to risks and dangers] *of false prophets, who come to you in sheep's clothing, but inwardly are ravenous wolves.*

V. 16-20 *By their fruit you will recognize them.* What kind of fruit do they produce? These comments by Jesus in verses 17-20 tell you to judge a prophet by the fruit they bear just like you would judge a tree by the fruit it bears. Does their character match up with what they are saying?

V. 21 *Not everyone* [including a so-called prophet] *who says to Me, "Lord, Lord," shall enter the kingdom of heaven, but he who does the will of My Father in heaven.* There is a "lordship" issue here.

V. 22-23 *Many will say to Me in that day, "Lord, Lord, have we not prophesied in Your name, cast out demons in Your name, and done many wonders in Your name?" And then I will declare to them, "I never knew you; depart from Me, you who practice lawlessness!"* A lot has been done in the name of the Lord that did not originate with Him, and He will neither overlook nor condone it.

V. 24 The next word is "therefore." The word "therefore" is used to introduce a logical conclusion. What we do with this teaching determines our foundation. Will we be wise? Rain, floods, and winds are coming and will beat upon our house, which is our life. *Therefore, everyone who hears these words of Mine and puts them into practice is like a wise man who built his house on the rock. The rain came down, the streams rose, and the winds blew and beat against that house; yet it did not fall, because it had its foundation on the rock. But everyone who hears these words of Mine and does not put them into practice is like a foolish man who built his house on sand. The rain came down, the streams rose, and the winds blew and beat against that house, and it fell with a great crash* (verses 24-27).

We must stay balanced. Our focus regarding prophets cannot primarily be on the *warning* concerning false prophets and what can go wrong. If we do this, we face prophets with fear and mistrust instead of faith. Jesus gave the instruction because He intended the foundation of His Church to be on the ministry of the apostles and prophets. The Apostle Paul teaches about this in his letter to the saints in Ephesus: *He [Jesus] came and preached peace to you who were far away and peace to those who were near. For through Him we both have access to the Father by one Spirit. Consequently, you are no longer foreigners and aliens, but fellow citizens with God's people and members of God's household,* **built on the foundation of the apostles and prophets, with Christ Jesus Himself as the chief cornerstone.** (Ephesians 2:17-20)

Jesus wanted His followers to know there was a way to judge the prophet to see if they had an intimate relationship with God. Their works would reveal that. There are those whose works do not come out of their relationship with Him. This reveals lawlessness, iniquity, and evildoing, and that their deeds originate in the carnal nature.

13

JESUS PROPHESIED

It was a very interesting study for me to see what prophetic words Jesus spoke. These words were sometimes to an individual, to His disciples, to the nation of Israel, and to what would become the Body of Christ.

Following Are Three Prophetic Words He Gave Peter

- He prophesied to Peter how, through a miracle, he would get the money to pay the tax: *"But so that we may not offend them, go to the lake and throw out your line. Take the first fish you catch; open its mouth and you will find a four-drachma coin. Take it and give it to them for My tax and yours."* (Matthew 17:27)

- After Peter vowed his loyalty to Jesus at the last supper: *"I tell you the truth,"* Jesus answered, *"this very night, before the rooster crows, you will disown Me three times."* (Matthew 26:34)

- Concerning Peter's death: *"I tell you the truth, when you were younger you dressed yourself and went where you wanted; but when you are old you will stretch out your hands, and someone else will dress you and lead you where you do not want to go." Jesus said this to indicate the kind of death by which Peter would glorify God.* (John 21:18)

He Prophesied to the Body of Christ

- Jesus prophesied that we would do greater works than He did! *Most assuredly, I say to you, he who believes in Me, the works that I do he will do also; and greater works than these he will do, because I go to My Father.* (John 14:12 NKJ)

- He prophesied about the reward for those who give up things for His sake: *And everyone who has left houses or brothers or sisters or father or mother or children or fields for My sake will receive a hundred times as much and will inherit eternal life.* (Matthew 19:29)

- He prophesied concerning Himself: after His time of testing, Jesus went into a synagogue and read Isaiah 61 and prophetically declared His calling. *The scroll of the prophet Isaiah was handed to Him. Unrolling it, He found the place where it is written: "The Spirit of the Lord is on Me, because He has anointed Me to preach good news to the poor. He has sent Me to proclaim freedom for the prisoners and recovery of sight for the blind, to release the oppressed, to proclaim the year of the Lord's favor." Then He rolled up the scroll, gave it back to the attendant and sat down. The eyes of everyone in the synagogue were fastened on Him, and He began by saying to them, "Today this scripture is fulfilled in your hearing."* (Luke 4:17-21)

- He prophesied about answered prayer and that He would be with those who gathered in His name: *Again, I tell you that if two of you on earth agree about anything you ask for, it will be done for you by My Father in heaven. For where two or three come together in My name, there am I with them.* (Matthew 18:19-20)

- He prophesied His arrest, suffering, and resurrection. *Now as Jesus was going up to Jerusalem, He took the twelve disciples aside and said to them, "We are going up to Jerusalem, and the Son of Man will be betrayed to the chief priests and the teachers of the law. They will condemn Him to death and will turn Him over to the Gentiles to be mocked and flogged and crucified. On the third day He will be raised to life!"* (Matthew 20:17)

He Prophesied to the High Priest

- *But Jesus remained silent. The high priest said to Him, "I charge You under oath by the living God: Tell us if You are the Christ, the Son of God. "Yes, it is as you say," Jesus replied. "But I say to all of you: In the future you will see the Son of Man sitting at the right hand of the Mighty One and coming on the clouds of heaven."* (Matthew 26:63-64)

He Prophesied Concerning His Followers

- *For John baptized with water, but in a few days you will be baptized with the Holy Spirit.* (Acts 1:5)

- *But you will receive power when the Holy Spirit comes on you; and you will be My witnesses in Jerusalem, and in all Judea and Samaria, and to the ends of the earth.* (Acts 1:8)

- *For whoever exalts himself will be humbled, and whoever humbles himself will be exalted.* (Matthew 23:12)

- *Therefore, the kingdom of heaven is like a king who wanted to settle accounts with his servants.* [This story is about forgiveness, and the last line is a prophetic word.] *This is how My heavenly Father will treat each of you unless you forgive your brother from your heart.* (Matthew 18:23, 35)

- Although the beginning of the Beatitudes says that He opened His mouth and began to teach them, it was prophetic in nature. He was prophetically declaring things that were conditional. (See Matthew 5:1-12.) Verse 7 says, *Blessed are the merciful, for they will be shown mercy.* He was prophetically declaring blessings that had a stipulation attached to them.

- In Matthew 5:17-19, He said that He did not come to abolish the Law or the Prophets, but to fulfill them. Then He made a prophetic declaration in verse 18: *I tell you the truth, until heaven and earth disappear, not the smallest letter, not the least stroke of a pen, will by any means disappear from the Law until everything is accomplished. Anyone who breaks one of the least of these commandments and teaches others to do the same will be called least in the kingdom of heaven, but whoever practices and teaches these commands will be called great in the kingdom of heaven.*

There are many more prophetic words that Jesus spoke. This was just a sampling of them. I reached the conclusion that He was extremely prophetic.

14

QUESTIONS ANSWERED

What Is Prophetic Evangelism?

Prophetic evangelism is when the prophetic gifting is used to touch those outside the Church. It can be through interpreting a dream for them or telling them something that the Lord tells you to say.

What is different about this kind of evangelism? There may not be the opportunity to follow-up with the person. It is done in obedience to the Spirit, and the results are often just left in His capable hands.

There is an example of this in Scriptures. In the book of Acts, there is the story of Philip ministering to the Ethiopian eunuch. He did what the Lord told him to do: led the man to the Lord, baptized him, and never saw him again. (Acts 8:26-40)

The intent is to bless individuals with the love of God. We may be planting a seed, watering it, or harvesting. It is up to the Lord.

Prophetic people can use the gifts the Lord has equipped them with to speak into the lives of spiritually hungry people. This is called prophetic evangelism.

What Do You Do With What You See?

This is potentially a problem with prophetic people. First, there is the questioning of oneself, "Why am I so critical?" Then there is the question of, "How come everybody else does not see what I see? It is so obvious!"

1 Corinthians 12 has a great teaching on the fact that there are many members of the body. Being eyes or ears means that we will see things that others do not see and hear things that others do not hear. One of the first things that will come up is – can God trust us?

Can He Trust Us in the Following Areas?

- To not blab what we see?

- To pray for what we see?

- Have we become mature enough *not* to "build a case" against people?

- Are we mature enough not to leave the church or ministry we are involved with?

- Will we continue to love people?

Common Mistakes That Seers Make:

- Thinking we are to tell everything we see. At first, I thought, why else would God show me something if I am not to share it?

- Confronting people with what we see.

- "Delivering the mail" when it was not intended to be delivered. We thought it was a message from the Lord, but it was something to pray about.

- Not praying it through before presenting it. It is a good thing to pray for the person we have a "word" for to prepare them ahead of time to be able to receive it.

- Taking a false responsibility for it and the person's reaction to what we tell them. A mail carrier only delivers the mail. It is not up to him to be sure a person opens it and reads it and pays the bill.

- Failing to walk in humility and having a "God told me" attitude. Our "word" can be accurate, but it is possible for a person to reject it because of our attitude.

- Getting offended because someone does not take us seriously when we see something. Not everyone sees what we see as prophetic people. And, it is possible that another prophetic person does not see what we see.

The majority of what we see prophetically will strictly be for prayer.

Are Women Called to Serve as Leaders in the Body of Christ?

Most Christians agree that women can serve as teachers, missionaries, and leaders over children and other women. This means they have the opinion that women can be *used in ministry*. It may be difficult for some to accept that God would give a woman a place of *spiritual authority*.

In a church congregation, over twenty years ago, we were told from the pulpit that God did not call women to the five-fold ministry. The pastor went on to say, "I realize there have been women that God has used, but it is because a man would not obey God and respond to the call on his life. It was not His perfect will to use her."

This disturbed me and caused me to search for what the Bible had to say. I came to the following conclusions:

- That comment turned out to be the opinion of a man.

- The Scriptures teach that there is a specific role for male and female in the family. *Wives, submit to your husbands as to the Lord. For the husband is the head of the wife as Christ is the head of the church, His body, of which He is the Savior. Now as the church submits to Christ, so also wives should submit to their husbands in everything. Husbands, love your wives, just as Christ loved the church and gave Himself up for her.* (Ephesians 5:22-25)

- There is an obvious difference in male and female, emotionally and biologically. However, there is neither male nor female in Christ. *There is neither Jew nor Greek, slave nor free, male nor female, for you are all one in Christ Jesus.* (Galatians 3:28)

Let us take a good look at this verse. It is saying that it does not matter who you are. The early Church discovered this firsthand. In the book of Acts, it is recorded that Peter was surprised when the Holy Spirit was poured out on believing Gentiles. He thought only Jews could be saved. *Then Peter opened his mouth, and said, "Of a truth I perceive that God is no respecter of persons"* (Acts 10:34 KJV). He then preached to them about Jesus. Then, *While Peter was still speaking these words, the Holy Spirit came on all who heard the message. The circumcised believers* [Jews] *who had come with Peter were* **astonished** *that the gift of the Holy Spirit had been poured out even on the Gentiles. For they heard them speaking in tongues and praising God. Then Peter said, "Can anyone keep these people from being baptized with water? They have received the Holy Spirit just as we have."* (Acts 10:44-47)

It is when the Spirit of God came on them that it was revealed Gentiles could be saved and baptized in the Holy Spirit.

Now concerning whether women only fill in for disobedient men when it comes to five-fold ministry, we must look to the Scriptures. The Lord planned our destinies in advance. *For we are God's workmanship, created in Christ Jesus to do good works,* **which God prepared in advance for us to do**. (Ephesians 2:10) God is the one who calls and chooses who He wants for different positions in His church. And **He Himself** *gave some to be apostles, some prophets, some evangelists, and some pastors and teachers.* (Ephesians 4:11 NKJ)

There are many women in this present day who are actively serving the Lord in ministry, but what about a Biblical example of a woman in ministry?

In the Old Testament, there is Deborah. *Deborah, a prophetess, the wife of Lappidoth, was leading Israel at that time. She held court under the Palm of Deborah between Ramah and Bethel in the hill country of Ephraim, and the Israelites came to her to have their disputes decided.* (Judges 4:4-5) She was serving in the office of prophet and judge for the nation of Israel. She had the word of the Lord for Barak to take ten thousand men and go into battle. He was willing to go into battle only if she went with him. He commanded armies – he was not a weak man. He wanted the prophetess to go with him because she had the word of the Lord. It took both Deborah and Barak to go to war and obtain victory. The Lord in this day will put together apostles and prophets to gain the victory over the enemy. There is neither male nor female. It is the anointing that makes the difference.

In the New Testament, one example is Priscilla. I will give a little background first. The first mention of this woman is in Acts 18:1-2. Paul tells about meeting a Jewish couple that came from Italy. *After this, Paul left Athens and went to Corinth. There he met a Jew named Aquila, a native of Pontus, who had recently come from Italy with his wife Priscilla, because Claudius had ordered all the Jews to leave Rome. Paul went to see them, and because he was a tentmaker as they were, he stayed and worked with them.*

In Romans 16:12, Paul says in a letter to greet Priscilla and Aquila, *my fellow workers in Christ Jesus.* By this it is revealed that along with being tentmakers, both man and wife were involved in ministry. There are seven references to this couple. Six of the seven times, Priscilla's name is mentioned first. The Scriptures say that the church met in their home. The mentioning of Priscilla first was to acknowledge her leadership, and it is believed that she was the pastor. I will explain. In our culture it is quite common to say the names of a man and wife in either order. For example: "Sherry and Mike" or "Mike and Sherry." In the New Testament days when these people were living, especially to show respect to the one who would be the leader, the name of the leader would be mentioned first. For instance, when the man who would become an apostle (Paul – formerly Saul of Tarsus) was paired up in a team with Barnabas, notice whose name was mentioned first in the writing. *The disciples, each according to his ability, decided to provide help for the brothers living in Judea. This they did, sending their gift to the elders by Barnabas and Saul.* (Acts 11:29-30)

Later on:

> But the word of God continued to increase and spread. When Barnabas and Saul had finished their mission, they returned from Jerusalem, taking with them John, also called Mark. While they were worshiping the Lord and fasting, the Holy Spirit said, "Set apart for me Barnabas and Saul for the work to which I have called them." So after they had fasted and prayed, they placed their hands on them and sent them off. (Acts 12:24-25)

They traveled and preached and when they came to Paphos, Paul confronted a sorcerer who was hindering his ministry, and the man was temporarily struck blind. (See Acts 13:2-3.) From this time forth, Paul's name is mentioned first because he had increased in authority and was now the leader of the ministry team.

Then Paul and Barnabas answered them boldly. (Acts 13:46)

But the Jews stirred up the devout and honorable women, and the chief men of the city, and raised persecution against Paul and Barnabas, and expelled them out of their coasts. (Acts 13:50)

At Iconium Paul and Barnabas went as usual into the Jewish synagogue. There they spoke so effectively that a great number of Jews and Gentiles believed. (Acts 14:1)

The anointing of God is going to surprise people in our modern day as God confirms, in an obvious way, His call on women to lead in places of authority in the Body of Christ.

15

GO FISHING

The very first memory of my childhood was catching a fish when I was four years old. My father was fishing in Biloxi, Mississippi off a big seawall. To occupy me, he took a piece of string and tied a tiny hook on it, so I could "fish," too. Of course, there was no bait on the hook because I was not *really* fishing. After a period of time, as I dangled my string with the hook, I actually snagged a little fish. When it wiggled, I was so excited that I took off running, which dragged the little fish up the seawall and through the sand five feet behind me as I was running and yelling, "I got one! I got one! I got one!" I made my daddy cook that little fish, and he told me years later with a smile, that there was hardly anything left after he cut off the head because it was so small.

Some people love to fish, but it has never interested me. I do not like to get my hands dirty, and I am not patient enough to enjoy this leisure sport. It is interesting that God would choose to speak to me in a dream about fishing.

I dreamed that a little girl had taken me by the hand, and we were at a Fall Festival like churches and schools have. We came to the "Go Fishing" area. She wanted both of us to do it. I humored her by taking a pole and paid twenty-five cents each for us to "fish." I was very skeptical that we would catch anything since there was not even any bait on the hook. I looked down at the shallow crystal-clear water and did not even see a minnow. However, I dropped my fishing line into the water, not expecting *anything* to happen. The next thing I knew, there was a *huge* fish on my line. The hook had snagged its gaping mouth, and it was not even resisting. I gently pulled, and it was coming in easily. I began to sing "I got it! I got it! I got it! I got it!" (a Judy Jacobs song declaring her faith and victory). I awakened.

The dream was so vivid that I could not quit thinking about it. It strongly impressed me that in the dream I was not expecting anything to happen when I went "fishing." I also knew by the Spirit that the little girl represented the young prophetic ministry that was developing at my church. The verse of Scripture that came to my mind was about when some fishermen had been fishing all night and had not caught anything. This story is recorded in Luke 5. Jesus was standing by the Sea of Galilee and He was teaching. Some fishermen were washing their nets, and He got into one of the boats to use it as a speaking platform. He asked the owner of the boat, Simon, to cast off from the shore. The acoustics were great over the water, and as His voice carried, everyone could hear Him well. After His message to the people, He told Simon to go out into the deep water and let down his nets in order to fish. Simon told Him that they had tried to catch fish all night long and did not catch anything.

Simon then said something very important, *"**Because You say so**, I will let down the nets."* When he and his helpers let down the nets, they caught so many fish that their nets began to break. They called their partners over in the other boat to help them, and the fish filled both boats, and they began to sink. When Simon Peter saw this, the fear of God came over him, and he fell on his knees and told Jesus to get away from him, for he was a sinful man. These guys were astonished at the catch of fish. Then Jesus said to Simon, *"Do not be afraid; from now on you will catch men." At this point they pulled their boats up on shore, left everything, and followed Him.*

The Lord let me know through this dream that even though I have fished for years and caught nothing, He is ready to bring in the big fish. He also let me know the big fish are willing to be caught. As I was praying about this dream, I had an exciting time in the Scriptures as I discovered a "big fish" that Jesus caught. The story is in John 4, and is commonly known as "The Woman at the Well." Jesus had gone into a village in Samaria and sat down by Jacob's well. He got into a conversation with a Samaritan woman when He asked her to give Him a drink of water. After much discussion about thirst and water, He asked her to go get her husband. She said, "I do not have one." He then told her that she was right and (at that moment began to operate in His prophetic gift) told her that in fact she previously had five husbands, and the man she had now was not her husband. This definitely got her attention, and she recognized that He was a prophet. Let me interject here that this is how prophetic evangelism is supposed to work. Then they got into a discussion about worship, she found out He was the Messiah, and she went back to town without her water pot and began telling everyone, *Come, see a man who told me everything I ever did. Could this be the Christ?* (John 4:29) Many of the Samaritans from that town believed in Him because of the woman's testimony, *He told me everything I ever did.* They urged Him to stay in the city for two days. During that time many more became believers. *They said to the woman, "We no longer believe just because of what you said; now we have heard for ourselves, and we know that this man really is the Savior of the world."* (John 4:42)

Right in the middle of this story, while the woman had run back to town, the disciples returned from buying food, and Jesus said to them that the harvest is *now*. He went on to say, *others have done the hard work, and you have reaped the benefits of their labor* (John 4:38b). In this present day, we just need to get in on what God is already doing.

The full interpretation of the dream was that there are big fish that are ready because God has used other people to prepare the way. *One sows and another reaps. I sent you to reap a crop for which you have not toiled.*

Other men have labored and you have stepped in to reap the results of their work. (John 4:37b-38 AMP) The reaping we are about to do is to harvest what others have sown. It will be as easy as picking the fruit at harvest time. It is work, but the fruit is ripe. Prophetic evangelism is going to bring in a harvest. He is saying to us that the harvest is ready now. Not only is the harvest ready, but "big fish" will facilitate a great harvest. Who are the people who are connected to so many lives? It is amazing that many people believed because of this "big fish" sharing her testimony with them. But many more believed because of the door that was opened up for the Lord to minister Himself.

The effects of true prophetic ministry on unbelievers can be: *But if all prophesy, and an unbeliever or an uninformed person comes in, he is convinced by all, he is judged by all. And thus the secrets of his heart are revealed; and so, falling down on his face, he will worship God and report that God is truly among you.* (1 Corinthians 14:24-25) God is so awesome! What a plan He has to reach people!

You might want to pray this prayer:

Lord, use me to bring in the end time harvest. Teach me how to move in the gifts of the Spirit and to be sensitive to Your leading. In Jesus name. Amen.

16

SOME THINGS I OVERCAME IN MY RELATIONSHIP WITH THE LORD

And without faith it is impossible to please God, because anyone who comes to Him must believe that He exists and that He rewards those who earnestly seek Him. (Hebrews 11:6)

Faith vs. Feelings

To be honest, I have waited on a feeling at times to see if God and I "connected." Then, if I did not have a feeling, I lacked faith to continue to press in. It made a difference when I began to have a daily scheduled time. I would continue because it was *our* time, not because I felt anything.

If you need a breakthrough in this area, here is a prayer to pray:

I plead the blood of Jesus over me. Lord, I am here because of Your faithfulness. I am here because You initiated this relationship. You sought me, drew me, and convicted me of my sins and my need of forgiveness. You saved me! You want to talk to me and for me to talk to You. This is a wonderful relationship that You ordained for us to have. Now, I am not waiting on a feeling. I am here by faith. My faith pleases You. I renounce unbelief and doubt and repent for allowing them to influence my life. I come to You this morning because I am welcome in Your presence. I choose to believe it! I am here because I am responding to the love You have shown me. You have been patient with me. I want to know You and to learn of You. I take Your yoke upon me.

Afraid of Being Honest with God

Intimacy is sharing heart to heart and being able to tell someone about our true feelings. When we are afraid to do this, we are limited in how close we can be in a relationship. Many people are out of touch with issues that need to be dealt with, and I was one of them. It was a very significant day when, at the Lord's prodding, I faced the issues I had not dealt with in all my years as a Christian. I had never admitted to myself, much less to God, that I was disappointed and hurt by things He had allowed to happen in my life. I *knew* He had the power to have prevented these things. He very lovingly had me empty one thing at a time from my barrel of unresolved issues. I forgave Him, and He healed me with the words He spoke to me.

Choose to take the time to get alone with the Lord to be honest with Him about how you feel. He knows it already. You will not shock Him. Tell Him if you are disappointed or feel that He let you down. Forgive Him and ask for healing.

Spiritual Laziness

Recently I said to the Lord: "I have come to spend time with You. What do You require from me?" He said, "Look up the word "lazy." This is what the Webster dictionary said: 1) unwilling to work or use energy; 2) showing or characterized by a lack of effort or care.

I realized that the Lord was pointing out to me that I was spiritually lazy. So, I took the definition and confessed my sin.

I prayed and repented like this: "Lord, I have shown a lack of effort or care. Help me. Lord, I confess to You that I have been spiritually lazy and have been unwilling to work or use energy spiritually. I repent and ask You to enable me to change." Grace is what enables us to do what we cannot do on our own.

Nugget: When you spend time with the Lord, have a dictionary handy. Many times the Lord speaks very simply, and you get the fuller meaning from looking it up.

Time with God

The next hindrance I had was not knowing what to do to have a "time with God" daily. First, I thought the problem was that I did not *have* or take the time to sit down and focus. But then even when there was time, I was not peaceful enough to be still and let my mind settle down. There was too much traffic in my head to focus and listen or even to worship.

These Things Helped to Have a Breakthrough

- Fasting.

- Sharing a prayer request with a friend to be praying for me in this area.

- Certain music stirs me spiritually. That helps.

- Praying aloud helps me to focus and keeps my mind from wandering off somewhere.

- Humbling myself and acknowledging my total dependence on the Lord.

Problems in Hearing God's Voice

- I had to learn to discern the Lord's voice as it came through my thoughts, impressions, circumstances, and the inner still small voice.

- I found out I had "selective" hearing. I tuned out what I did not think I could do or wanted to do.

- I discovered that obedience played an important role in hearing the voice of God.

- Through experience, I began to discern who was speaking: the enemy, me, or God.

- I found out that just like there are some young people who think they know everything already, I could be just like that. How many of us are "teenagers" in maturity concerning the things of the Spirit? Can God tell us anything? Do we have a problem with authority figures, too?

- There had been times that I thought that God was speaking, and when I "obeyed," found out it was not Him. I prayed for healing and deliverance from confusion and fear of "missing it" again.

17

DITCHES

God has called us to walk on the Highway of Holiness. To do so takes trust and obedience. If we stay on that highway, we experience growth and progress. No one told me that I had a very real enemy who would do what he could to keep me off the road. Strategically placed on each side of this narrow highway are ditches that are very easy to slide into. From my experience, here are a few ways that I glided off the road. I first started out in the "zeal without knowledge" stage (Romans 10:2). Freshly baptized in the Holy Spirit, I was ready to lay hands on somebody and heal his cancer right then. What started all this was that the Lord was performing some amazing things in my family. My toddler had injured herself twice and been miraculously healed. Also, my husband was dismantling a boat and as he swung the sledge hammer, he missed the target entire and slammed into his shin as hard as he could. He immediately cried out to God knowing he had just smashed the bone, and he looked down and there was not even a scratch or bruise to show for it.

I was so impressed with God's ability to intervene in the natural realm that I even came up with some ideas on my own. I was not aware that these were my own ideas. Hey, it seemed like God to me! I was a real novice at this point and I figured God was looking for faith. So I even commanded the rain to stop once – it did not stop. I gave money away to get God to pay off some bills for me – He did not do it. I even mailed off checks "in faith" that God would supply the money before they hit the bank. I quoted all the "give and you will receive" verses I knew. This was not a big success either. Looking back now, I see that these disasters led me to back off from expecting the miraculous. I had been sabotaged in my faith. Sabotage means to disable, undermine, or damage. I had slid off the highway in the ditch called PRESUMPTION. I had the rude awakening that God is under no obligation to do something that does not originate with Him. I really did not know what to do with these disappointments, so I just pushed them down in my barrel of unresolved issues and forgot about them as I crawled back up on the highway.

I cannot say that I was walking on the Highway of Holiness at this point. Limping would be more like it. I moved into the "waiting on God" mode. Sure, I believed that what God said was true. Someday both the written Word and the prophetic words we had received would materialize. I knew that one day God would do what He had promised. It is amazing what a mindset can do for you. As I entered into "waiting on God," I became passive. This passivity was a counterfeit "rest." So, I slid off into the ditch of PASSIVITY on the other side of the road to wait. The passive ditch kept me off the highway of growth and progress. Time went by and I reassured myself that I believed what God had said and one day it would happen. The only problem I was having was that people who had been saved years after me were getting what God had promised *me.* This led me to get out my big flashlight and begin morbid introspection. Looking inward, I found plenty to be disgusted about and worked on myself without much success. Then I heard someone say, "You are not waiting on God, He is waiting on you." Aha! I do not belong in this ditch. Yeah, you are right if you think I decided to get in there and do something to help matters along. I slid back into the PRESUMPTION ditch, added some more items to my unresolved issues barrel, and went on. What a frustrated and defeated life I was living!

I had no idea of my condition. Thankfully, God intervened in my life through someone under the prophetic anointing. He told me that I had traded *intimacy* for *ministry* – which really meant I traded my relationship and time with the Lord for religious activity. I cried and cried as I faced this. Then, I backed out of all religious activity other than attending church. I focused on restoring our relationship and had amazing results.

Religion and not hearing the voice of the Lord caused me to get into first one ditch and then the other – passivity and presumption. Jesus taught a parable about Himself as the true shepherd. One of the things He said was, *My sheep listen to My voice; I know them, and they follow Me.* (John 10:27) Lambs have to learn to hear it. And when they are mature they will know His voice. The Scriptures say, *You will hear a voice behind you saying this is the way, walk in it.* (Isaiah 30:21) Without that voice, there is no way to stay on the straight and narrow road. We must be able to discern the Lord's voice above our own and all the others that clamor to be heard both in the seen and unseen realms.

The enemy's goal is to get us to move in presumption and then, since it did not work, to then decide to just passively wait on God. Any method that will keep us in a ditch is a success for him. There is a living, fresh walk with the Lord that He has called us to. It is painful at times to stay on the path. It is lonely sometimes to say on the path, but if we keep our eyes straight ahead on Jesus, we will reach our destination.

18

SPIRITUAL CHALLENGE

God continually works in my life to change my way of thinking. Here is a parallel to illustrate my point. I usually have a good ole pair of shoes that will go with nearly all my outfits. They are my favorites because they are so comfortable. They are stretched out in all the right places, and I am completely unaware of them when they are on my feet. There comes a time when they begin to look worn and tired, and it is time to break in a *new* good ole pair of shoes.

When I pick the new shoes, they look good, but they sure do not feel as comfortable as the old ones. But, because I care what I look like, I know I must move on to the new pair and I really like how they look on me. However, I find that there are four things that will hinder me in making the change to the new pair:

- Compromise – Because I want comfort the most, I will slip on the old shoes over and over to run a quick errand and put off breaking in the new pair.

- Double-mindedness – One minute I am feeling a little ashamed of my worn shoes and wanting to break in the new pair, and the next thing I know, I am choosing comfort again.

- Apathy – There are times that I do not care if I ever make the change.

- Procrastination – I know that I will make the change, but it seems that it will not be today.

"Religion" and my old way of thinking are the old pair of shoes. God keeps calling me up to higher ground, which is a new walk as the result of a renewed mind. Those old patterns of thinking just will not "get it" anymore, and I *know* it. I cannot walk in unbelief and doubt anymore. I must walk in faith. Have you ever thought about how comfortable doubt and unbelief are? Faith will take you right out of your comfort zone. I cannot be double-minded, apathetic, compromising, and procrastinating. If I do not get rid of my old shoes, I never will walk in newness of life.

19

DIFFERENT PROPHETIC EXPRESSIONS

The following are different prophetic expressions. Keep in mind that prophetic means to do things by divine inspiration, to predict, or speak for God.

- Prophetic Acts – Things done in obedience to the Lord that have tremendous significance in the spirit realm.

- Prophetic Movement and Gestures – God says to the unseen world, "This is what I [God] intend to do."

- Prophetic Art – Work that is divinely inspired and carries a message.

- Prophetic Counseling – The majority of counseling is where the one being counseled does a lot of talking about his or her problems to reveal to the counselor what the difficulties are.

Prophetic counseling is Spirit-led and totally dependent on the Lord to reveal root problems, and wisdom is given then on how to bring freedom.

- Prophetic Dance – This is when a message from the Lord is conveyed through the movement of the dancer.

- Prophetic Deliverance – The Holy Spirit reveals what a person is ready to be delivered from, and they are set free.

- Prophetic Drama – A visual parable that demonstrates the message.

- Prophetic Evangelism – Prophetic evangelism is when the prophetic gift is used to touch those outside the Church.

- Prophetic Intercession – Intercession is prayer on behalf of others. There are times when a person is praying and the anointing (a special grace from God) comes on the person to pray and declare things he or she hadn't intended or thought about praying beforehand.

- Prophetic Song – This is when a person either sings by divine inspiration to the Lord or allows the Lord to sing through him or her to someone else. The singing is unrehearsed and is usually heard for the first time by the singer as it comes forth from his or her mouth.

- Prophetic Teaching and Preaching.

- Prophetic Word – This can be spoken or written, to individuals or to a corporate body.

EPILOGUE

The cool thing about God is that we get to experience Him and His kingdom. This is not religion. It is life! It is one thing to read about it and another to live it. It takes faith to apply the things that were written and shared through *Prophetic Boot Camp*. I pray you experience more and more freedom to be what God called you to be!

I like the way the Apostle Paul signed off on his letter to the Corinthian church, and this is my prayer for you. It contains three keys.

> May the **grace** of the Lord Jesus Christ, and the **love** of God, and the **fellowship** of the Holy Spirit be with you all.
> (2 Corinthians 13:14)

Grace – It takes lots of it to walk out our salvation, to mature, and bear fruit.

Love – Faith works by love. The more we become secure in God's love and understand His love for people, the more we can stretch and exercise faith and move into the greater works Jesus told us we would do!

Fellowship with the Holy Spirit – It will change us daily and give us the confidence we need.

I wish you *Godspeed*.

ABOUT THE AUTHOR

Sherry Anderson is a teacher and writer with a strong prophetic anointing. She is passionate about God's kingdom and wants to see the army of the Lord rise in boldness and stand with perseverance. She mentors others in the prophetic, teaching them to hear the voice of God, to understand His ways, and interpret dreams.

Sherry has been a leader both in Aglow International and the church for many years. She presently is the State Leader for Aglow in Florida. She and her husband, Mike, live in Panama City, Florida.

RECOMMENDED READING AND TRAINING

Basic Training for the Prophetic Ministry by Kris Vallaton (available in book, study guide, DVDs, MP3 downloads, and Kindle).

School of the Prophets: Advanced Training for Prophetic Ministry by Kris Vallaton (all available as above).

Developing Your Prophetic Gifting by Graham Cooke.

REFERENCES

Chapter 1 – Quote from Graham Cooke.
This quote was taken from an Internet announcement regarding a conference he was holding in California in 2005. (http://www.grahamcooke.com/conferences.htm, August 10, 2005).

Chapter 12, p. 58 – Definition of "Reward."
Merriam-Webster Online, http://www.m-w.com/dictionary.htm, (Accessed September 19, 2005).

Chapter 16, p. 85 – Definition of "Lazy."
Webster's Universal College Dictionary (2001, 1997), Random House.

Epilogue, p. 100 – Origin of phrase "Godspeed."
"Middle English god speid, from the phrase God spede you God prosper you: a prosperous journey: success." Retrieved from Merriam Webster Online Dictionary, http://www.m-w.com/dictionary/Godspeed (Accessed December 3, 2005).

References marked "Webster" are from Webster's Universal College Dictionary (2001, 1997), Random House.

References marked "Webster's 1828 American Dictionary" are from Webster, Noah. American Dictionary of the English Language (2 Volumes; New York: S. Converse, 1828).

Made in the USA
Columbia, SC
08 June 2023